Police Officers

by Nancy Dickmann

raintree

Raintree is an imprint of Capstone Global Library Limited, a company incorporated in England and Wales having its registered office at 264 Banbury Road, Oxford, OX2 7DY – Registered company number 6695582

www.raintree.co.uk
myorders@raintree.co.uk

Produced by Brown Bear Books Ltd:
Text: Nancy Dickmann
Design Manager: Keith Davis
Editorial Director: Lindsey Lowe
Children's Publisher: Anne O'Daly
Picture Manager: Sophie Mortimer
Printed and bound in India

ISBN: 978-1-4747-5549-8 (hardback)
21 20 19 18 17
10 9 8 7 6 5 3 2 1

ISBN: 978-1-4747-5553-5 (paperback)
22 21 20 19 18
10 9 8 7 6 5 3 2 1

British Library Cataloguing in Publication Data
A full catalogue record for this book is available from the British Library.

Acknowledgements
We would like to thank the following for permission to reproduce photographs:
Alamy: Campsie News 13, Charles Dye 12, Janine Wiedel Photolibrary cover, Jeff Morgan 03 20;
Dreamstime: Martin Brayley 19; Getty Images: Edmond Terakoplan/AFP 7; istockphoto: 1, 10, CS fotoimges 16, Amanda Lewis 5t, Andrewa Road 4, John F. Scott 5b, 15; courtesy Lochardil Primary School 21; Courtesy of the Mayor's Office of Policing and Crime 11; Rex Features: Photofusion 9; Shutterstock: 1000 words 6, Expose 14, LongJon 17, Machael Puche 8; Thinkstock: Chris Mueller 18

Brown Bear Books has made every attempt to contact copyright holders of material reproduced in this book. Any omissions will be rectified in subsequent printings if notice is given to the publisher. If anyone has any information please contact licensing@brownbearbooks.co.uk

Contents

Some words are shown in bold, **like this**. You can find out what they mean by looking in the glossary.

We need the police

There are many people who help us. Police officers help us. There are police officers in your local **community**.

Police officers keep us all safe. They make sure that people obey the **laws**. They work with us to help make our communities safer.

What the police do

For a police officer, every day is different. They have many kinds of jobs to do.

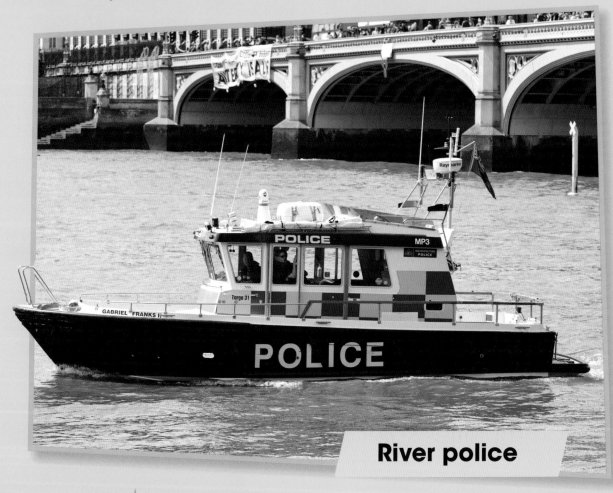

River police

Police officers solve **crimes** and catch **criminals**. They also help out in different types of **emergencies**.

On duty

Police officers **patrol** the local **community**. People are less likely to break the law if there are police officers around.

Police officers get to know the people in their area. Knowing the community helps them do their job better.

Solving crimes

A **crime** is when someone breaks the **law**. A **criminal** might steal a car. He or she might break into houses to take things.

People call the police when something is stolen. The police do their best to find the criminal. They interview people and search for clues.

Emergency!

If there is an **emergency**, the police will come to help. It might be a road accident, or a fallen tree.

Police officers can give **first aid**.
They make sure people get help.
Police officers keep people away
from danger.

Keeping order

Police officers work at football matches, parades and other big events. They make sure everyone in the crowd stays safe.

Mounted police officer

Traffic control

Some police officers direct traffic.
They keep drivers away from
dangerous or crowded areas.

Police uniforms

It is easy to spot a police officer. They wear **uniforms**. They often wear **high-vis jackets** as well.

Radio

Police officers carry radios. They use them to talk to other police officers. They also carry tools such as **batons** and sprays to keep themselves safe.

Police vehicles

Police officers must travel quickly in an **emergency**. Their cars have lights and **sirens**. These warn other drivers to let them pass.

Some police use motorbikes when they are on duty. Other police officers ride bicycles.

Police in schools

Police officers often visit schools. They talk to children about their job. They explain how they help the local **community**.

Speed camera

Police officers teach children how to stay safe. Officers talk to children about what to do in an **emergency**.

Staying safe

Always remember:

🚓 The police are there to help.

🚓 If you are lost or need help, find a police officer.

🚓 Do not talk to strangers, or go anywhere with them.

🚓 Call 999 in an emergency.

Glossary

baton stick used to protect against attack

beat regular route that a police officer patrols

community particular area where a group of people live

crime something a person does that is against the law

criminal person who commits a crime

emergency serious situation, such as a fire or road accident, that calls for fast action

first aid emergency medical help given while waiting for a doctor

high-vis jacket bright, reflective jacket that makes a person easy to see, even in the dark

law rule that everyone must follow

patrol to guard an area by making regular trips through it

siren warning device that makes a loud noise

uniform special type of clothing worn by all members of a group, such as the police

Find out more

Books

Call the Police (In an Emergency), Cath Senker (Franklin Watts, 2013)

Police (Popcorn: People Who Help Us), Honor Head (Wayland, 2012)

Police Officer (Busy People), Lucy M George (QEB Publishing, 2016)

Police Officer (People Who Help Us), Rebecca Hunter (Tulip Books, 2014)

Websites

safestreet.west-midlands.police.uk

Test your safety knowledge

www.bbc.co.uk/schools/citizenx/national/crime/lowdown/crime_ basics_1.shtml

Find out more about police and crime laws

Index